AF365742

TRUTH OF PEACE AND WAR

PEACE DESIGN

A GUIDE TO END CONFLICT AND CREATE PEACE

HANAKO • FRITZ LENSCH

CONTENTS

WELCOME

BY HANAKO

Life has its battles, whether within ourselves in the form of illness or throughout entire nations at war. I often ask myself, how am I going to deal with this? What can I do? Should I protest? Would I be able to join the resistance? I search for solutions and consider the possibilities. Then, I ask more fundamental questions, like, what is morality? What are my ethics? Only through those might I find a way to be at peace with war.

Fritz and I met through a renowned peace-builder. When I listened to her first lecture in Amsterdam, she asked the audience: *"If you want to do something about war, you need to be willing to die for it."* It hit like thunder. I knew this was the gateway to understanding how to find peace. As an educator, I was inspired to go more deeply into this. I was asked to teach on the subject together with Fritz at the Transmission School. That's what happened, and it became this book.

BY FRITZ

We tend to confuse peace with the absence of war. The belief is that we must resolve war in order to attain peace. The word *peace* comes from 'to fix,' but this doesn't seem to work. Wars carry on in our personal and collective lives. Healing may prevent war, but we still appear helpless in the face of it. There must be another way than to fight for, in, or against war. This is what Hanako and I set out to find. Our journey was to be with the conflict in ourselves and see how it could translate into war. We wanted to arrive at some kind of ultimate truth about peace and war beyond our own experiences and ideas. I knew this might illuminate our way forward. Through our work on Peace Design, we found how to deal with conflict without getting stuck in it.

I was very happy to meet Hanako, who turned out to be a true friend and partner in revealing the different layers of reality. For weeks, we met online and in Italy and Scotland on the quest for truth, or as Hanako would say, *'to dive for the pearl.'* We shared many discoveries and personal realizations going through our conflicts. What we found was astonishing. It made us feel more responsible yet lifted weight off our shoulders. The students in our Peace Design courses helped us bring out the magnitude of our findings. *Thanks to all of you!*

We looked up the word *war* (which we did with many of the words to find out their true meaning), and we were perplexed to find that it comes from 'to confuse.' We were not surprised by the definition, but that it was hidden in plain sight. Indeed, **war is a confusion of our true nature** and its natural principles and values. We are conditioned not to be in the present and not to accept ourselves as we are. We learn to accumulate experiences of the past in the pursuit of some future.

This is the manifestation of the ego, or as we call it, our sense of self. Followed blindly, we move away from our true selves and develop ideals that we come to protect and even fight for if necessary. When we blame ourselves or others for our ideals not being met, we move into conflict. This may be the beginning of a war.

When we realize our true nature, however, we can return back to ourselves to **find out what peace really is and who we really are**. This is our task now.

INTRODUCTION

OUR INSPIRATION FOR THE BOOK

Far removed from collective wars, it was difficult for us to discern what we could do about them. There was frustration in our respective approaches and methods for peace while remaining at peace ourselves. We could see that our frustration exacerbated the conflict, and we wanted to find a more effective way. We were asked to teach a course on this subject, which allowed us to inquire and investigate more deeply. We aimed to get to the bottom of war and peace so that we could put an end to all forms of violence in body and mind. We also wanted to find out where we stand on war and the type of action or inaction we could take to resolve it.

We share our discoveries in this book. It is a guide, with the same questions we asked ourselves, through a journey of awakening, liberation, transcendence, and perhaps realizing truth. Going through the steps in this book, we may see the source of conflict and create an opportunity to be free from it. This can be an awakening to a new energy field where there is no war at all. The conflict begins to dissolve, and light seems to shine brighter. There is silence, and we become available to life again, where action can flow freely.

These discoveries are new, but they originate from ancient texts. You might be familiar with them intellectually, but we elaborate on their application in this book. Once the simplicity of what we share comes through, it may impact all areas of life.

RELEVANCE

We all want to create peace in our lives. It's hard to imagine a single person who wants conflict or war for *themselves.* But all too frequently, we find ourselves in it. The suffering leaves traces on our body, heart, and mind, as well as our soul. The damage is beyond measure. It's reflected in our wars and continuing conflicts that are influencing us every day. Many of us watch and experience them in agony over our own futility. Our strategies for peace are clearly inept since we remain in constant cycles of conflict. Entrenched in our fixed mindsets, we produce the same results, individually and collectively, with only marginal changes over time. Our lives are largely consumed by conflicts and the energy invested in them. Just imagine this energy invested elsewhere. We point to the source of conflict, empowering you to take action based on facts. This liberates new possibilities for life and potentially a world without war.

WHICH WARS

We use the term *war* when we are in conflict with the present moment. There is the belief that something is wrong, and the pursuit of peace justifies the means to get there. There are personal wars and collective wars. Here are a few examples.

PERSONAL WARS

At war with my body (illness, aging, death)
At war with my emotions (fear, anger)
At war with my thoughts (ego)

COLLECTIVE WARS

War for territory
War on nature (resources)
War of ideology (religious wars, war for peace)

Personal wars grow into collective wars when conflict and fear are projected onto others. We blame others for our suffering or blame it all on ourselves. Either way, we use conflict as a primal way of relating to ourselves.

For example, a business leader who fears the failure of their company creates a war for survival. So does a president of a country who fears their demise. Our inner conflict, in body, mind, and emotions, creates a war on Earth.

At this point in the book, we would like you to write down in a journal or notebook:

WHAT ARE YOUR PERSONAL WARS?

Investigate now: *What do you feel in a personal war?* The experience can be a kind of 'twistedness' in the stomach and a clouded mind, with agitation rising from below. It helps to become aware of the feeling to be able to recognize a personal war, allowing you to work with it.

WHO IS THIS FOR?

This book can be a guide to those who are looking to end conflict and create peace. For this, we ask you to keep track of the sensation of personal war. Conflict is first felt in the body before our minds can make sense of it. It may live on and manifest as an illness or a war if it remains unseen. Unresolved tension disturbs harmony. This book is a guide to releasing personal and collective tension. We investigate the source of conflict for this. As the saying goes, *this is simple but not easy*. Reading this material can feel uncomfortable, especially if one's life is invested in the illusion. Identification with suffering and having something to fight for provides a sense of meaning. We may be unaware of this identification and its costs. Otherwise, we would have long stepped out of it. There is a fear before we cross over into the unknown. In the eyes of a perceived threat to what we know, we may want to fight, flight, or freeze. But trust that there is a treasure for you to discover here.

HOW TO USE THIS?

The value of the book is in the inquiry and investigation. Close your eyes once in a while to feel what is true for you. This heightens the ability to receive and digest it fully. To start each chapter, we explore the title and provide some background so that we can have a mutual understanding of the word. This book leads us through *Questions to end conflict*. At the end of the book, after going on The Way of Truth through the stages of illusion, awakening, liberation, and transcendence, we added a visual map for the journey where you can follow each step of the way. Once truth is discovered, there is no longer a need for questions or a map to reach peace.

1 ILLUSION

WE EXPLORE THE WORD

An illusion obscures the perception of truth. We are often oblivious to it. We tend to view through the lenses of judgment, creating labels and stereotypes. They make ideas and beliefs that are ultimately not real or what they seem to be.[1]

"Although illusions distort the human perception of reality, they are generally shared by most people."[2]

In Latin, the word illusion comes from 'ludere,' which means 'to play.' This is like the harlequin performing a comedy. He deceives or mocks the audience.[3] The Italian theatrical character Pulcinella, for example, which we include because we were inspired to write the book in Italy, "either plays dumb, though he is very much aware of the situation, or acts as though he is the most intelligent and competent, despite being woefully ignorant."[4] He escapes death by playing on power and fear. His secrets are hidden in plain sight.

In Sanskrit, the classical language of India, illusion translates as 'Māyā.' The word later became a creation of a god. It was given the power of deception.[5] Here, gods are at play. Gods are created as manifestations of thought patterns.

The mind is deceiving us, not the gods, that we are separate from the divine.

This book specifically investigates the illusion of duality between war and peace, which has severe consequences.

THE ILLUSION OF DUALITY

Ideas of war and peace are likely to be quite different. They are often thought of as opposites in conflict. But there is no peace without war, and no war without peace. This may be difficult to grasp, but it is impossible to distinguish one term without the other. Try communicating about peace without war on your mind. War and peace are, in fact, not separate. They are one. This is the case with all dualities. The realization can be challenging at first. Just give it a moment to digest.

UNDERSTANDING THE MECHANISM OF ILLUSION

We now go through the illusion step by step to understand its mechanism. Later in this chapter, we will lay it all out on the **Peace Design Map**.

First, there is a *charge***.** The charge is an energy that is triggered by internal or external motions. This is not to be confused with emotions. Those are already mental interpretations of the charge. There is *war* when one goes into conflict with this charge, wanting it gone. The conflict starts internally with whether *'there is something wrong with me'* or *'something wrong with them.'* Either way, we may come up with ideals for how things should be. This is what is thought of as *'peace.'*

Strategies to get peace are created, forming a gap between what is happening right now and the future. Strategies are meant to reach the ideal of peace, but how they are used only fuels war. This is where we can get caught in the *field of illusion*, which causes suffering.

Here are two examples:

Example 1: The *charge* is an odd look or comment from one's mother or partner. This may give the feeling of "There's something wrong with me."

It creates internal *war,* which consists of feelings of shame, inferiority, abandonment, and anger.

The *strategies* to get peace are pretending, helping, being perfect, lying, manipulating, confronting, or hiding.

So *peace* can be achieved, which may be thought of as harmony or feeling loved.

Example 2: The *charge* is observing people killing each other. The thought follows, "There's something wrong with them."

War creates fear, heartbreak, sleepless nights, anger, wondering what to do.

Strategies for 'peace' are to ignore and hide or confront and fight. To make it stop.

The strategies create a field of illusion. They are dysfunctional in reaching the goal since they are carried out with conflict. For example, when we meditate to feel calmer, the meditation is already conflicted since we want something other than what is happening. Meditation is to be with what is happening. We may be unaware that we made an action into a strategy and justify their pursuit with the goal in sight. We chase it like a carrot in front of a rabbit. The game is endless.

In the name of peace, people are willing to sacrifice truth and fall prey to illusion.

EXTREME EXAMPLES

As we suffer the conflict with what is happening, the strategies for peace can become more severe. If the belief is, *'there is something wrong with me,'* we may try to escape — for example, by overworking, overconsumption, and other addictions. This is to compensate and numb into feeling better, which ends up being an illusion. More severe strategies include self-harm and suicide to release the suffering.

If the belief is *'there is something wrong with them,'* we may manipulate or blackmail to provoke a different behavior. Should it be necessary, some even choose to kill 'for the greater good.' This is how wars escalate.

In 2023, suicide was the second leading cause of death for 14 to 24-year-olds. Worldwide, there are 800,000 recorded deaths by suicide every year. That's one death every 40 seconds.[6]

Homicide, which counts as unlawful murder, accounts for 400,000 deaths. It doesn't include war deaths, which qualify as 'lawful murder.'[7] This shows the costs of the illusion at the personal and collective level. Yet we keep participating in it. Why?

WHY IT CONTINUES

We can ask ourselves this question once we have become aware of illusion. This is the first step in awakening. Conflict is the way of the ego to give meaning to itself. Our sense of self depends upon our mission. Therefore, we may never actually want the conflict to end. Relationships often survive on conflict. The goal of Peace is illusory. It gives us something to occupy ourselves with. Out of fear of emptiness, we long for stimulation and ways to 'fulfill' our sense of self – striving for something makes us feel alive. It gives a sense of meaning and purpose, even if we have to give and take suffering for it.

MANIPULATING BY ILLUSION

The illusion is often used for the purpose of manipulation. Our strive creates valuable energy. Manipulators capitalize on it by reinforcing the perception of dualities and then offering strategies for salvation. This strengthens its grip on us further. Examples are found in systems such as politics, religious organizations, and business advertising.

*"We are **doomed**. <u>Vote for me</u>, and there will be **bloom**."*

*"You are a **sinner**. <u>Join us</u> to become a **saint**."*

*"You are a **loser**. <u>Buy this</u> to become a **winner**."*

Our motivation to participate in the illusion is the prospect of achieving something or becoming someone. This has become somewhat of a driving force for society. The mechanism of manipulation is to generate suffering by using the conflict between polarities. There is a problem fabricated that is met with a solution. This is big business. The Global advertising industry is expected to exceed $1 trillion by 2025[8]. The aim is for people to be financially productive, not happy and at peace. True contentment is unprofitable. We have normalized such approaches, but their use is malicious. We use this word deliberately to point to the importance of our awakening. We are deceived into thinking that striving is the only way to achieve in life. But *there is free and infinite energy available.*

QUESTIONS

We share discoveries to be investigated for their legitimacy and truth. The following questions are meant to facilitate the revealing of the illusion. Please go through the questions carefully. Choose one personal or collective conflict that feels important. Sit with each question quietly and *feel* your answers. We invite you to reflect on the following questions and take some notes

WHO OR WHAT IS THE TRIGGER?

WHAT IS THE CONFLICT?

WHO IS WRONG IN THIS CONFLICT?

WHAT IS
PEACE FOR
YOU IN THIS
CONFLICT?

WHAT IS YOUR STRATEGY TO GET TO PEACE?

2 AWAKENING

WE EXPLORE THE WORD

As we become aware of the illusion, we begin to distinguish between what is true and false. This reveals the deceiving nature of ideas and strategies that manifest in thought patterns. The play of deception is out, and its secrets are obvious. The mind opens to new possibilities. This is where a new chapter begins.

In Old English, awakening is the "act of starting to understand or feel something."[9] It is a movement from inactivity and indifference to interest and attention.[10] The Latin translation of awakening, 'Evigilare,' means to "study with careful attention" or "watch throughout the night."[11] This resonates with the Sanskrit term 'Bodhi,' which signifies awakening due to insight and practice. It points to the truth of things. The term originates in '√Budh,' which means "to have woken up and understood."[12]

BENEATH SUFFERING

The gift of seeing clearly comes with exceptional power and responsibility. But it's up to us whether we want to act on it. The realization is the beginning of the journey, not the end. Prince Siddhartha, who later became known as the Buddha, was kept by his father, the king, inside the palace walls for protection. When he discovered suffering outside them, he escaped the palace to investigate how to end it. This is now our choice to make. Once we become aware of suffering, do we want to stay there or get to the bottom of it? Fear is the true reason why we may have not gone beyond yet. In the comfort of what we know, the unknown appears terrifying. But nothing is known. Comfort is a play whose backstage is collapsing. *The known is illusionary*. The mind fabricates it as an attempt to control reality. This is what we call a program.

If we decide to get to the bottom of suffering, we realize it as a program that has manifested deeply in our habits and beliefs. This program shapes who we think we are. It creates the world as we know it. These habits are reinforced by repetition. We might be so entrenched in the program that even if we recognize suffering, the force of habit keeps us going. This has been going on for generations and has become a bigger field of consciousness, for example, through parenting and education. Revealing our true nature brings life back to equilibrium.

DISCONNECTION FROM OUR TRUE NATURE

For this, we need to distinguish our true nature from the program. This is an important step in awakening. As the program manifests in habits and beliefs, it forms patterns of behavior that we can recognize in the following expressions:

- We get triggered by events that go against our ideas.
- We blame ourselves or others for what is happening.
- We manipulate to achieve our own ideas.
- We separate ourselves from others and their patterns.
- We look for allies with whom we share similar patterns to justify our own behavior.

If we get to the bottom of our thoughts, emotions, and actions, we can feel if they are true or part of a fabricated pattern. We use patterns, consciously or unconsciously, as strategies to alleviate suffering and get peace. This forms the illusion.

TRUE ACTION

Desire creates conflict. We have become used to chasing ideas. But our natural state is quiet and remains still, no matter the circumstances. If we can access this underneath the chaos, action can flow naturally.

We know what to do. We act on our intuition without fear or self-concern. There is no sense of self and, therefore, no agenda. Helping a child in an emergency is a no-brainer. However, the program often lays itself on top of our true nature, shutting down our intuition. It fabricates our idea of ourselves that we come to believe in and even fight for. As long as we remain unaware of this, our true nature will remain covered. In this case, we declare the idea of ourselves as the center of the universe. Habitual thoughts become our reference point for everything. The world turns into a film production of the program. The only reason why we are seeking something is to find our way back to that stillness of our true nature. But we have *already arrived.* We can access it anytime, anywhere.

BEYOND THE CHAOS

Of course, when a conflict breaks out, it is not an illusion. The situation is very real, but how it came about, and the reactions more often come from programmed behavior patterns. Knowing this, the question is whether we fall for it and create a strategy or come into the stillness of our true nature. There, we find ourselves beyond the chaos, where actions that are uniquely ours can emerge.

QUESTIONS

Continue investigating the same personal or collective conflict as in the previous chapter. The questions help us reveal more clearly our ideas of ourselves. Therefore, they require your full honesty and attention. Feel the truth within and keep digging until you discover the treasure.

WHAT IS
REALLY
AT THE
BOTTOM
OF THIS
CONFLICT?

WHAT IS IT
MADE OF?

WHAT ARE
YOU REALLY
PROTECTING?

3 TRANSCENDENCE

WE EXPLORE THE WORD

Transcendence is a leap into the unknown. We are going beyond thoughts and the words to describe them. We invite you on the journey from the surface of the program to the depth of our true nature. This is *the way*, or in Chinese, 'the Dao.'

The term 'transcendence' stands for the quality of being able to go beyond normality.[13] The roots in Latin are 'trans,' meaning *beyond*, and 'scandare,' meaning *to climb*.[14] This is often interpreted as the attainment of the infinite state. We don't use it in this way but to describe the realization of our awakening. In Sanskrit, the simplest and most fitting translation for Transcendence is 'Pāragate,' which means *gone beyond*. This is beautifully captured in the final lines of the Heart Sutra, a central scripture in Mahayana Buddhism:

gate gate pāragate pārasaṃgate bodhi svāhā

This translates to: "Gone, Gone, Gone Beyond, Gone Utterly Beyond, Oh what an Awakening."

Sanskrit offers multiple interpretations of the word. Pāragate can mean 'having departed from the world,' as in transcending the program, but it can also mean 'having returned.' We understand this as returning to our true nature. If actions emerge from stillness, they dissolve back into it.

THE FIELD OF LIBERATION

When we can be with what is happening in the present moment without fighting it, the field of liberation opens. Here, we allow the charge to move through. In the field of liberation, there is nothing wrong and no one to blame. We can be with a problem without any problem. We are no longer under the force of the program.

TRANSCENDING THE CONFLICT

This is a precious moment in the book when we can experience the charge and let go of our personal resistance to it. Rather than going into our usual behavior patterns to avoid feeling, we can transcend our conflict with what is and move into action. We suggest going through a process of feeling the charge, which can be quite intense. Go slowly and take enough time for each step.

Start by initiating a charge. Think of the conflict used for the questions earlier or another situation that triggers an internal reaction.

Now, close your eyes and allow the energy of the charge to move through. Keep any reactions inside and give it no resistance. Breathe in and out and create space for it to flow without labeling anything.

Feel what is happening with full attention. Add no further reaction or thought to it. Continue to let it play out without playing it any further.

Leave everything as it is. This is important. Entering the eye of the storm may be intense. But when the storm clears, we know exactly where we are and what to do.

Surrender all resistance to what is. Give no further thought to it. The pain of fighting conflict eventually drops away. We are left with the pure energy of the charge. It becomes our free and infinite fuel for action.

Take as much time as needed, or return to the practice later. If any resistance remains, there will not be this experience yet. Silently watch all reactions until they come to an end.

With the clouds passing, we may transcend our conflict with what is. Now we can see more clearly what to do. We can recognize truth and act upon it. This is not based on our inner commentary or external causes but simply on the facts of our knowing. We gain back the energy that was lost in strategies. This is the power of liberation. We are in harmony with ourselves and the world. There is no more war left in us.

STRATEGIES VS. ACTIONS

Strategies and actions may be the same in performance. However, it's their intention that distinguishes them. We react to experiences by making a strategy to fulfill a goal. Strategies are means to an end, following the logic of cause and effect. Their underlying agenda may be intentionally calculated or unconscious.

Actions, on the other hand, are taken with integrity to what we know. There is no hidden agenda. This may seem alien to our sense of self from which we think in terms of our benefit and protection. Actions are not always serving that.

Actions alone are pure and effective, but when thoughts of our sense of self infiltrate them, they can quickly turn into strategies — this is where we may loop back into conflict.

LOOPING BACK INTO CONFLICT

If we allow self-serving thoughts to lead our actions, they become part of a plan. When the plan does not work out, we may resist the charge and loop back into conflict. The way beyond this is to allow the charge to move through, giving nothing but our full attention. When we finally let go of our resistance, even the resistance itself, and surrender without giving in, there is no war left to fight.

The stage of transcendence is distinct from truth because there is still a way back into conflict. Our identification with the outcome of our actions keeps us suffering. Stepping over to the other shore is surrendering completely.

We return to our true nature when action is taken with integrity, not in pursuit of a goal. We are living out truth. We can see our own nature everywhere, even in the suffering. We may still be part of the program but no longer feed it.

THE AFTERMATH OF LIBERATION

Having crossed over to the other side, we may provoke a reaction from people. These reactions can be strategies intended to bring us back into the program. Since we act contrary to habits and beliefs, we may trigger anger or fear. We might be perceived as a threat.

If the program wants to be like us, however, we may be admired instead. We may be identified and celebrated as a leader, teacher, or reformer. The story of Jesus is a good example of this. He was feared by authorities who wanted to retain control and admired by the followers who longed to become like him. Very few actually revealed and lived his message.

QUESTIONS

We recommend to investigate the same conflict as in previous chapters. This allows us to walk through the entire life cycle of conflict. Our resistance must be resolved before we can answer the following questions truthfully. If we still find ourselves lost in stories, it is best to go back to **the process** earlier in the book to clear the charge before reading on.

WHAT ARE THE FACTS OF THIS CONFLICT?

HOW DO YOU KNOW THESE FACTS?

WHAT IS
THE ACTION
TO TAKE
TO BE IN
INTEGRITY
WITH THE
FACTS?

WHAT ARE YOU TAKING THIS ACTION FOR?

WHAT
IF THIS
DOESN'T
WORK?

If we can truly let go of our attachment to the outcome, the weight is lifted off our shoulders. This has to come naturally, though, rather than by our own doing, which would be another strategy. If there is the slightest twist in the stomach answering the final two questions, we advise returning to the questions in chapter two to get to the bottom of the conflict.

4 TRUTH

WE EXPLORE THE WORD

We can start this chapter by asking, 'What is truth?'

The question already gives us the answer. Truth is *what is*. When we see what is happening and be with it, we are in touch with truth. This reveals many layers of reality manifest in our thoughts, feelings, and behaviors. In the light of this moment, truth shines through the silence of our essential nature. The Sanskrit word 'Satya' also translates into essence, which is unchangeable. We can personalize truth, as in 'my truth,' into a virtue of truthfulness and authenticity, as well as into personal understanding of knowledge. The truth, however, is definite. As we see and live through our conflict with what is, it may dissolve, and our face can brighten up again amid any situation. Words are not the truth, but they can point you to it.

ARRIVING IN TRUTH

As we arrive in truth, seeing things as they are, resistance to what is happening has dissolved. We emerge from conflict with the light and radiance of true peace. This is our true and essential nature. It has always been there, only buried underneath the reality of the program. As we see through the programming of our body, mind, and emotions, habitual thoughts and their strategies can come to an end. The conflict can still be there, but we are no longer fighting it. **The conflict ends with us**. This is an irreversible discovery we can return to when triggered again.

AVAILABILITY

From our essential nature, we can see truth beyond words and appearances. We feel what is a fact and what is not without our sense of self getting in the way. Our thoughts, words, and actions can be simple and straightforward. Life may unfold naturally without an agenda. It is no longer the consequence of something or someone else but remains alive and new. We can see truth everywhere. Even pain guides us there. We find it in a genuine smile and behind tears, in the first snowflakes and the cold, in leaves whirling in the wind and a tree falling from old age. Its nature may put a smile or a tear on our face. These are divine drops.

CREATION

The essential silence of our mind restores natural order. It cleans out the program and holds balance and harmony. There is no need to control anymore since the implications and fears of our sense of self, with a chaotic mind, have disappeared. We no longer depend on authority since we have become fully responsible for ourselves and the world. Intuition is the compass of action. Creation emerges from silence. It is divine, and we can discover it in some music, in a painting, in a dance, in flowers, or while cooking. From silence, we can do what the program has declared impossible. Terminal illnesses may disappear, impossible relationships may be reinstated, and mountains may be moved. There are many stories like this if there is an openness to hear them. With a smile, we like to call it *pulling a Jesus*.

THE DIVINE

Miracles emerge from this emptiness, where there is nothing in particular. This is not logical, but that's exactly what we understand a miracle to be. It cannot be planned. In the empty space of the unknown, possibilities of the divine can manifest. It brings a profoundness of being that leaves us in awe of life. We can see the program with a divine laugh. We have stepped out, and what remains is complete harmony and perfection.

ONE FINAL QUESTION

Now, further investigate the last question of the previous chapter: *What if this doesn't work?* Be aware of body sensations that arise. If we still feel a charge, the transcendence of war is not complete, and we're back at the beginning of the journey.

If you feel no attachment to the outcome, genuinely, absolutely, truthfully, then you are liberated. So check your answer with this question:

DO YOU
KNOW
WITHOUT
A DOUBT
THIS TO BE
TRUE?

5 THE WAY OF TRUTH

AWAY IS NOT THE WAY

There are painful moments and peaceful moments in everyday life. Beyond right and wrong, bring awareness to whatever is happening without fighting it. Actions can emerge naturally as a consequence of knowing truth. The way of truth is not to avoid or bypass conflict but to go all the way to the end of it. We must recognize conflict and investigate its source until it disappears. We return to the silence of our essential nature.

The realization is that illusion is also part of truth. This is another duality to transcend. We need the illusion to recognize what is true. Illusion can be seen as divine orchestration for being free. The pain of conflict moves us along the way until we discover the end of it.

Conflict is a symptom of an unresolved charge. When energy gets stuck, it manifests in painful conditions such as an illness or even a war. Energy can flow again when we walk on the way of truth, allowing ourselves to do the work. Blockages dissolve, and things go back to their natural state. Rivers clean themselves when we allow them to flow without interference. Dolphins came back to Venice, and foxes back to London, when cities came to a still. Wars stop when the people fighting them put down their weapons.

OUR JOURNEY TOGETHER

Peace is not something we can do, and then we're done. It's not a service or a product. There is no beginning and no end. We are *'the way.'* Our light touches the world and reflects back upon us. The world comes alive again and starts to talk to us. It brings joy, prosperity, and longevity.

STAYING IN TRUTH

We still get charged by events, but we are able to go beyond the conflict with them. We allow whatever energy to move through us and are able to see beyond. This ability needs maintenance. If we let thoughts come in between us and what is happening, we create separation again and re-enter the field of illusion. Only when we drop the thoughts, witnessing without labels, can we continue to dwell beyond. This is true power. We remain innocent and impenetrable to influence. Staying in truth, we are not getting hooked back into the program.

We naturally remain still if we see the costs of going against the present moment and the tension this creates. We are not ignoring the charge but allowing it to move through without feeding it. In this way, our actions can align with the truth, regardless of the consequences. This requires tremendous courage and discipline. We have to cultivate our own energy to be able to match the charge. This comes through everything, from the food we eat, the clothes we wear, and the products we use – to the relationships we are in. They reflect what we are and can support us in standing our ground. There are no rules for this other than our feeling of what's right for us. If we're truly honest with ourselves, it will come back to us through honest things and people.

The following quick questions can guide finding what aligns with our essential nature. Choose a relationship, service or object to investigate. Let the answers be simple and straightforward.

What is this relationship/service/object made of?

How was it made?

Do you truly love him/her/them/it?

If we don't truly love it, *drop it*. If we truly love it, there is the power to transform it, even when there is pain. A relationship can be transformed by one moment of true connection. A product can be transformed by truly feeling it. A service can be transformed by seeing truth behind the appearance.

TECHNOLOGY AND MEDIA

The worlds fabricated by technology and media may pull us out of our feeling of truth. This can also be a mechanism of manipulation. If we don't pay attention, technology and media confuse our consciousness, influence our thoughts and condition our behavior. We get distracted and pulled into their frequency if we don't hold our center. We may start to live in a fictional reality and lose touch with what is. Certain personalities are being worshipped as modern-day gods. We idolize or demonize their character as the heroes or villains in our story. But if we become more or less like the idea we have of them, we sacrifice parts of ourselves and move away from our essential nature.

Systematically, technology enters our body and mind. For example, the amount of energy that comes through the phone leaves traces that we may not be aware of. These traces can alter our dreams and change our condition. Our attention becomes increasingly absorbed and unavailable to life. This literally changes our reality. The implications are far worse than assumed. Overconsumption of media is a form of hypnosis when we get lost in their worlds. The stimulation changes the alchemy in our body, which affects our constitution. It influences our nervous system and triggers certain emotions and reactions that rule us to live in a certain way. The study of this book is to find out *who we really are*. In our essential nature, technology and media has no effect on us anymore. This is when you are free to use technology and media without the need for it – like birds don't need a map to find their way.

6 COLLECTIVE WARS

When we are no longer under the influence of a personal charge, we can see the world from a different point of view. We are able to surrender our position when we take the 'I' out of the picture. Either directly or indirectly, we are still confronted with wars in the world every day. But our relationship with them changed. When we write down all the collective wars that we can think of, the list becomes overwhelmingly long. This includes long ongoing wars such as:

Military and ideological conflicts, such as between the West and Russia;

Political wars on terror and drugs;

Sexual violence, such as child abuse and the oppression of women and sexuality;

Class conflicts, such as between Elites and People;

Local wars between communities, neighborhoods, and families.

This is not a complete list or an exercise in gathering them all. We want to feel the quality of the field created by collective wars without getting lost in it. This can be very challenging, but it's important not only to intellectualize war but to understand the real impact it has on us. We may feel the 'naked' feeling, allowing the charge to move through. But more often than not, we then identify with a certain role in the conflict. For the purpose of this work, we suggest two particular roles: *the victim and the perpetrator*.

Review the list above and ask yourself: Who am I in this conflict – the victim or the perpetrator? See how fast we take one of these roles in any given war.

Feel the charge of this particular role. This may provide a motor to step out of our identification with it.

You may even be willing to take the opposing role and feel its impact. This could be hard, but it is necessary to realize that both roles are equally devastating. They only play themselves out, adding to the continuity of war. Only when we recognize and understand this can our relationship with war change. We see that everyone loses. This truth is revealed to our heart. The charge stuck in the identification can only now transform into universal compassion.

Compassion becomes our fuel for peace.

7 QUESTIONS AND PEACE DESIGN MAP

This is a summary of all our questions about transcending conflict and creating peace in any situation, both personal and collective. Afterwards, we share our Peace Design Map. It illustrates the journey we have been taking together, leading through each step of the conflict. Alongside the questions, it may help to understand war and experience peace.

WHO OR WHAT IS THE TRIGGER?

WHAT IS THE CONFLICT?

WHO IS
WRONG
IN THIS
CONFLICT?

WHAT IS YOUR STRATEGY TO GET TO PEACE?

WHAT IS
REALLY
AT THE
BOTTOM
OF THIS
CONFLICT?

WHAT ARE YOU REALLY PROTECTING?

WHAT IS THE ACTION TO TAKE TO BE IN INTEGRITY WITH THE FACTS?

WHAT ARE YOU TAKING THIS ACTION FOR?

WHAT IF IT DOESN'T WORK?

DO YOU
KNOW
THIS TO BE
TRUE?

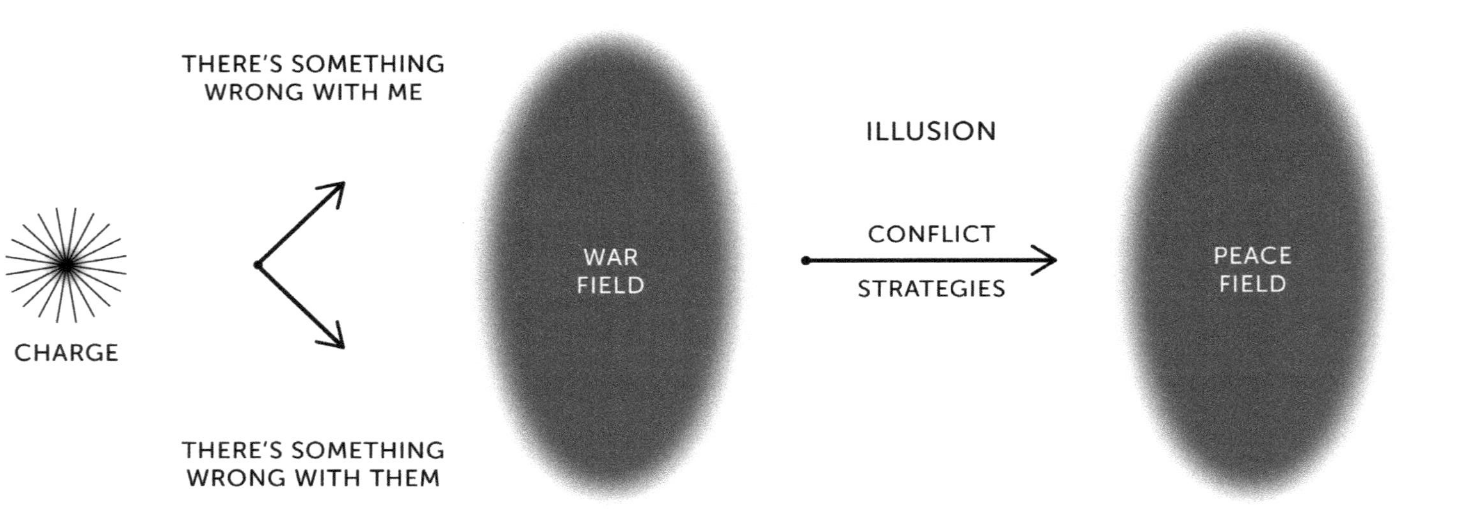
CHARGE
THERE'S SOMETHING WRONG WITH ME
THERE'S SOMETHING WRONG WITH THEM
WAR FIELD
ILLUSION
CONFLICT STRATEGIES
PEACE FIELD

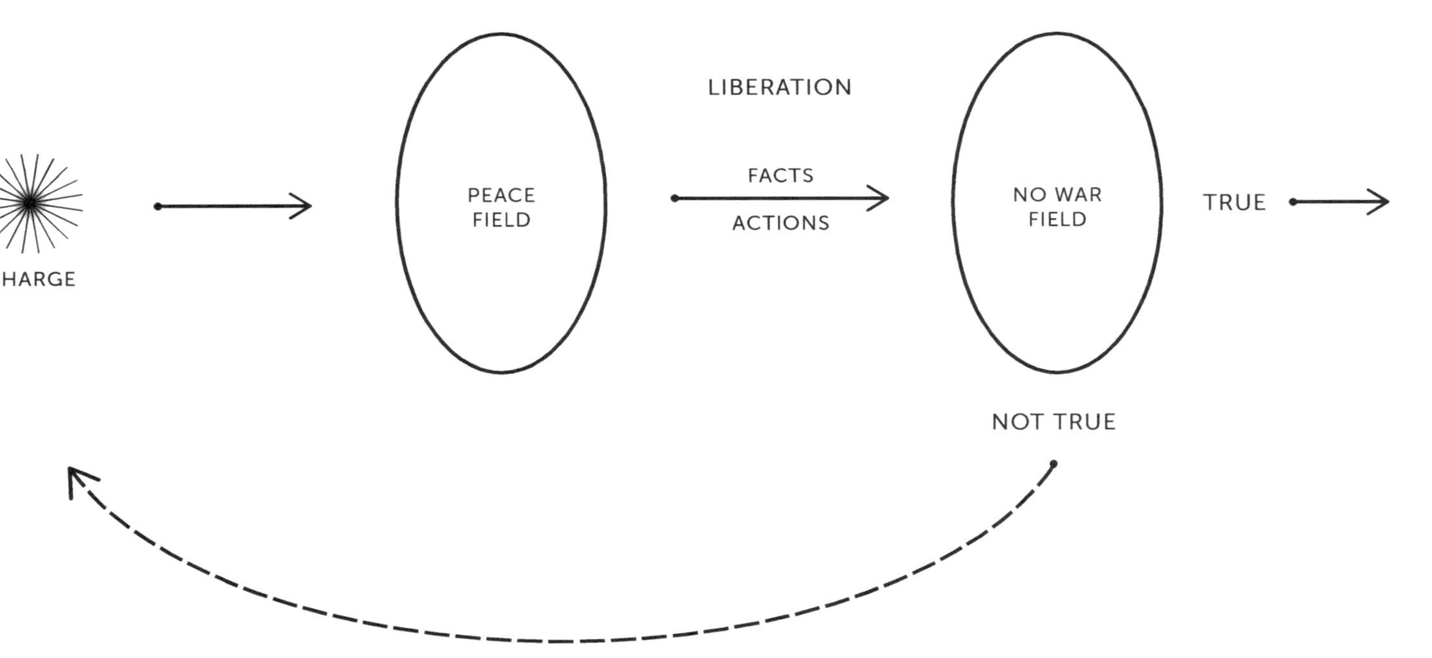
CHARGE
PEACE
FIELD
LIBERATION
FACTS
ACTIONS
NO WAR
FIELD
TRUE
NOT TRUE

ACKNOWLEDGEMENTS

We would like to thank The Transmission School in Italy for asking us to teach on the subject, Judith Volker for encouraging us to share our discoveries with the world, Justine July Giordano and Melanie Ena for editing and helping us shape the book, and Mary O'Neill for the design and artwork.

NOTES

[1] Illusion [Internet]. [cited 2024 Mar 27]. Available from: https://dictionary.cambridge.org/dictionary/english/illusion

[2] Illusion [Internet]. Wikimedia Foundation; 2024 [cited 2024 Mar 27]. Available from: https://en.wikipedia.org/wiki/Illusion

[3] Falsehood [Internet]. [cited 2024 Mar 27]. Available from: https://www.etymonline.com/word/falsehood

[4] Pulcinella [Internet]. Wikimedia Foundation; 2024 [cited 2024 Mar 27]. Available from: https://en.wikipedia.org/wiki/Pulcinella

[5] Maya [Internet]. [cited 2024 Mar 27]. Available from: https://www.britannica.com/topic/maya-Indian-philosophy

[6] Suicide statistics and facts [Internet]. 2023 [cited 2024 Mar 27]. Available from: https://save.org/about-suicide/suicide-statistics/

7 Herre B, Spooner F, Roser M. Homicides [Internet]. 2023 [cited 2024 Mar 27]. Available from: https://ourworldindata.org/homicides

8 Kelly C. Global ad spending on track to top $1T for first time, WARC says [Internet]. 2023 [cited 2024 Mar 27]. Available from: https://www.marketingdive.com/news/global-ad-spending-2023-2024-1t-trillion-warc/692010/

9 Awakening [Internet]. [cited 2024 Mar 27]. Available from: https://dictionary.cambridge.org/dictionary/english/awakening

10 Awakening definition & meaning [Internet]. [cited 2024 Mar 27]. Available from: https://www.merriam-webster.com/dictionary/awakening

11 Evigilare translation from Latin to English [Internet]. [cited 2024 Mar 27]. Available from: https://mymemory.translated.net/en/Latin/English/evigilare

12 Bodhi [Internet]. HandWiki; 2022 [cited 2024 Mar 27]. Available from: https://encyclopedia.pub/entry/35075

13 Transcendence definition and meaning [Internet]. [cited 2024 Mar 27]. Available from: https://www.collinsdictionary.com/dictionary/english/transcendence

[14] 1. Transcendence - definition, meaning & synonyms [Internet]. [cited 2024 Mar 27]. Available from: https://www.vocabulary.com/dictionary/transcendence.

9 783982 667102

Indigenous Games Played in the Khasi and Jaintia Hills of Meghalaya, India

Indigenous Games Played in the Khasi and Jaintia Hills of Meghalaya, India

By

Andriana Pyngrope,

Bikika Laloo Tariang &

Rumika Talang

Vij Books

New Delhi (India)

Published by

Vij Books
(Publishers, Distributors & Importers)
4836/24, 3rd Floor, Ansari Road
Delhi – 110 002
Phone: 91-11-43596460
Mobile: 98110 94883
e-mail: contact@vijpublishing.com
www.vijbooks.in

Copyright © 2024, *Authors*

ISBN: 978-81-19438-11-2 (PB)

CONTENTS

PREFACE

Almost every community in India practices its own unique recreational activities and that includes the Khasis and Jaintias of Meghalaya, India. For centuries, the Khasis and Jaintias have been playing games like Mawpoin, Sohtyngkoh, Hai-iu and others. Sadly, as with other types of indigenous knowledge, many of the traditional games played by these tribes too are disappearing into oblivion, owing to the demise of the practitioners, the disinterest of the younger generation in practicing and propagating the games, the onslaught of offline and online foreign games and the lack of documentation of the indigenous games. The authors attempted to document the prominent indigenous games played by the Khasis and Jaintias, in consultation with custodians and participants of this unique Indigenous knowledge. Various such indigenous games are described, step wise, accompanied by photographs, to substantiate the text. A book of this nature would be of interest to indigenous and non-indigenous readers and is expected to pique the interest of social scientists and travelers as well. Additionally, it would further go a long way in bringing visibility to the Khasi and Jaintia tribes of Meghalaya.

The authors would like to thank all the contact persons from the Khasi and Jaintia Hills for their valuable contribution to this book.

CHAPTER 1

INDIGENOUS GAMES AND THEIR SIGNIFICANCE

While there is a surge in modern knowledge, owing to research in all disciplines, traditional or indigenous knowledge, owned and practiced in certain pockets of the world, is in danger of extinction, being as it is, still largely oral and also due to the lack of interest among the younger generation in propagating such valuable knowledge. Along with other categories of indigenous knowledge and practices, many indigenous games are also losing their significance, owing to the same problems mentioned above. Only a few groups, particularly those based in rural areas, still faithfully indulge in such games. Considering the many benefits of indigenous games, such as for example, their contribution to physical and mental health as well as their low cost, a call for their documentation is long overdue. This work attempts to document the indigenous games that were and are prevalent with a tribal community in the North Eastern region of India.

Indigenous Games

Indigenous games are recreational activities that originated from a particular cultural group, community or people. These games are different from your mainstream sports, which are regulated by international federations, and have fixed rules. Conversely, indigenous games do not have internationally regulated rules for implementation; local organisers determine these according to the customs of the local participants. This creates many different versions of the same game. Indigenous games are a very important part of a people's heritage and culture. They preserve age-old traditions and stories of the people group. (Ndiko, 2018)

According to Farreira (2014) "Indigenous games are part of the symbolic patrimonial heritage of indigenous peoples…. Accounts of the first voyagers and missionaries in the 16th century described how games were part of sacred ceremonies and rituals, which involve tension and excitement. In numerous accounts and interviews about games that are still being practiced today, we can note characteristics related to time: the games represent a break in everyday activities and point back to a mythical time, with a union between the individual and the cosmos, moments of transformation, a passage from one state to another, and emotions, such as pleasure, joy, sadness, pain, fear, anger and triumph. It is important to reinforce the idea that indigenous time is based on a different paradigm, which is cosmological and seasonal. In the past, colonisers considered indigenous ceremonies and rituals to be demonic and barbaric because they were not compatible with occidental cultural models. For this reason, many rituals and games were forced into oblivion and disappeared. The effects of globalisation and the distancing of today's people from their ancestors' traditions are also harmful to the preservation of traditional games."

Significance of Indigenous Games in India

The history of traditional games in India is very ancient and with its origin in early Vedic era (2000-1000 B.C.). Games have been an important part of Indian culture endlessly right from their origin. India is considered as a place of origin for a number of traditional games which are well-known throughout the world in present time. A number of leading traditional games which had Indian origin are Teerandaji, Kabbadi, Kho-Kho, Polo, Shatranj and Martial Arts. All these games require technical and tactical skills, along with other physiological components like speed, strength, stamina, agility and coordinative abilities. Apart from this, our traditional games require very little equipment and they are less expensive, in comparison to the modern games, and as a result, traditional games of Indian origin became more popular amongst the masses. Yet much needs to be done at the government level so that they can be well promoted and Indians can retain their glorious heritage. (Gulia, and Dhauta, 2019)

Significance of Indigenous Games in Meghalaya

Meghalaya, a state in the North Eastern Region of India, is basically made up of the three distinct ethnic communities called the Khasis, the Jaintias and the Garos, along with smaller sub groups. Meghalaya is rich in traditional knowledge and best practices practised by indigenous tribes in which many of them are of age old traditions. Many of these knowledge and practices were closely related to their livelihood. With modern technology especially in agriculture, such practices have gradually depleted from the community (Bio-Resourcce Development Centre, Shillong). Indigenous practices are still being followed in some of the everyday activities of the tribes in Meghalaya. These include agricultural, food and health indigenous practices. Indigenous sports and games have been played in Meghalaya for centuries now, some have been lost to oblivion due to the negligence from the indigenous practitioners themselves, while most of the urban folk have been taken captive by online games. Some of indigenous games are still being played, but mostly by the rural folk, especially rural children.

CHAPTER 2

INDIGENOUS GAMES PLAYED BY CHILDREN IN THE KHASI HILLS DISTRICT OF MEGHALAYA

Indigenous games existed since time immemorial in Meghalaya and the knowledge has been passed on from one generation to another. Most of the identified games which were known to be popular in the past are now forgotten. While some of them still remain, they are played irregularly and are mostly played by children in rural areas.

Different games were played in different parts of the Khasi Hills. Some of the games played by children have common methods and rules while the names of the games are different. Sometimes the names of the games may be identical while the way of playing is different, that is, the rules and the constraint are different in some places of the Khasi hills. The most popular games that are played till today are the games called "*mawpoin*", "*mawkynting*", and "*siat khnam*" (archery, also called "*teer*").

A survey was carried out using questionnaires and interview. The questions pertained to various aspects of the indigenous games, such as the categories of indigenous games; items used in each games; the number of participants in each game; the categories of participants for each game; the rules and regulations governing each game; preservation of each game; etc.

Identifying key contacts

Before undergoing the above method, key contacts were firstly identified through word of mouth or the snowball sampling method, starting with the people known to the researchers. Key contacts are important people who are experts or have experience in the field, and who can provide relevant information about the study. Then the questionnaires were distributed. Interviews were also conducted, to gain more information. The following were the Key people involved for this part of the book:

i.   Contact Number 1 – Mr. Lambha Kurbah (one of the researchers' father) - who has personal experience in playing different indigenous games in his childhood.

ii.   Contact Number 2 – Mrs. Cecilia Pyngrope (one of the researchers' mother) - who has experience in playing different indigenous games in her childhood.

iii.   Contact Number 3 - Prof. Streamlet Dkhar - Professor in the Khasi Department, North Eastern Hill University, who has experience and knowledge regarding the different indigenous games that were and are played by children in the Khasi Hills of Meghalaya

iv.   Contact Number 4 - Mr. Robert Star Lyngdoh - a guest lecturer in the Khasi Department, North Eastern Hill University, who has knowledge about the different games that he himself played during his childhood.

v.   Contact Number 5 -   Miss Yavonnie Diengdoh - Assistant teacher in Khasi, in a Government Girls Higher Secondary School Shillong, who has experience in playing different indigenous games in her childhood.

vi.   Contact Number 6 – Mrs. Sweetymon Rynjah - a writer/ author of many books related to the culture and heritage of the Khasi People.

vii.   Contact Number 7 – Mr. Damang Syngkon - District Sports Officer, South West Khasi Hills, who has formulated rules for mawpoin and also organises mawpoin competitions

Based on the data collected from the respondents (key people), the following are the identified indigenous games that were/are popular in the Khasi Hills district of Meghalaya.

Lehkai kot sikret/ iathong kot sikret/ pashat kot sikret

This is a type of game played by both male and female children, where raw materials such as unused cigarette packets and rubber slippers (flip flops) are used.

Firstly the cigarette packets are torn in such a way that they resemble card pieces. Then a small circle called "in" is drawn on the ground. The players will then bet among themselves how many cigarette cards will be kept inside the circle. For example, if there are 5 players and if they decide to put 2 cards each then the total number of cards inside the circle will be 10.

After the bet has been done, the cigarette cards are then put inside the circle. The next step is to draw a line near the circle. All players who want to play the game will firstly throw their slippers from the circle towards the line. A player whose slipper reaches near the line will get the chance to attempt the game first and is also referred to as the first player and thus the position and numbering of players will go on.

The first player will then throw the slipper towards the centre or the ''in" in such a way that the cigarette card must come out of the ''in". The second player will also try to do the same followed by the rest of the players. If the first player could make the cigarette card come out of the in, he or she will get to keep the card. The game will go on till all cards come out of the "in". The player who fails to make any card come out from the "in" is out from the game.

In some parts within the Khasi Hills district, some children and adults may also impose rules and constraints for this game, which are as follows:

1. If the thrown slipper falls inside the circle or the "in" then that player is out from the game.

2. While trying to make the cigarette card come out of the "in," if the slipper thrown by the player touches the slipper of the previous player then that player whose slipper has been touched by the other player will be out from the game.

Children playing Lehkai kot sikret

Dieng phlok/ siat siej

It is a type of game which mostly young children play. The raw material used in this game is bamboo, which is split into two layers. The outer layer and the inner layer of the bamboo act as a gun for shooting, and a piece of chewed up paper forms a bullet. There is no restriction on the number of players and they can be divided into two teams. The team that gets to chase will act as soldiers or the enemy and will shoot the opponent using this bamboo gun, till all players of the opposing team are shot. The game continues with the other team's turn to shoot the opponent, like soldiers.

Niah kali taiar/ niah lishien/ niah kali ring

This is a type of game where children use materials such as an old tyre of a vehicle or an iron, moulded into a ring, and a handle, usually made of bamboo, to steer the tyre or iron wheel . Players can be as many as possible and children usually play this kind of game on the roads/lanes where the players will have to steer or drive the ring or the tyre using the handle mentioned above. The one who can steer or drive the tyre or iron ring for the longest distance wins the game.

Lehkai khajih

Khajih means to catch by touching. It is an outdoor game. This type of game is mostly played by female children and teenagers. Firstly, before the game begins, two circles are drawn on the ground, a big and a medium circle, which will act as a home to the players, also called "ka iing" (house) in the Khasi language. Then the players will count among themselves, the one left out at the end of the counting will be the one to catch the other players. As soon as the players are done with counting and have a result of who will be chasing them, they all gather inside the big circle. The chaser will then roam round and round outside the circle such that he/she is able to catch or touch any of the players inside the circle. Anyone inside the circle who has been touched by the chaser will be out of the game and has to come out of the circle and become another chaser. This process will continue till all players are touched. At some point the players can move to the other circle to prevent themselves from getting touched by the chaser.

Lehkai kot dur

"Kot dur" means a photo or card. It is a type of game which resembles playing cards. The material used is mostly wrestling photos. The game is played by two or three players, depending upon the choice of the players. Firstly, the players will bet among themselves to decide which person starts the game. The game begins with the players laying the photos one after another. While laying the photos, if each player has the same wrestler photo name then the one who puts the photo last will get all the photos. The process will continue on and on. If the opponent has no photo left or if the opponent has less photos left and does not wish to continue in the game, then the other player wins and the game ends. In some part of the Khasi Hills district this game is still common.

Mareh da ki siej/lehkai iaid kulai

This is a racing challenge game mostly played by male children. The game involves 'riding' a bamboo stick and racing against each other. The bamboo is made in such a way that it has a foot handle where the player can put their legs. To be part of the game, a player must put both legs on the handle attached to the bamboo and dare to walk and run on it. The one who finishes the race first, wins the game.

Bsiat shyieng sohkyntoi

A game is mostly played by children of all ages (approx. above 12 years), "bsiat" means to strike and "shyieng sohkyntoi" means a tamarind seed. In this kind of indigenous game, children use tamarind seeds as tools/toys for playing. The game begins by spreading of the tamarind seeds on the flat surface (ground). Then children use their last finger to cross between the seeds as if making a line between them, and strike the seeds. The process continues till all seeds get struck. Once the striking is done, the next step is to lift the seed into the back of the palm and calculate the number of seeds that fall on the back of the palm.

Rules and constraints

1. The seed/s are not allowed to move while making a middle line/ partition between them.

2. Once a seed moves, the player is out from the game.

The game will end when there will be a winner with the leading scores.

Dienghai/ Diengkhun

Dienghai/Diengkhun was common in the Khasi Hills in the olden times. Both male and female can play the game. But mostly boys were fond of playing this game, as it involved physical strength. "Dieng" has many meanings; it can be a whole tree or a branch of a tree or even a piece of wood, "hai" means to chase, "Khun" has two meanings; one could be an offspring and the other meaning could be to steer. The raw material used were branch/ branches of tree, or wood. The name of the game is so called, could be because of the material used or could be due to the process in which it was played. Before the game started, a somewhat rectangular hole was made on the ground. The hole measured about 10-15 cm. The players would then decide among them, who would get to play first. The first player would begin the game by putting the short/small piece of wood in between the hole so as to create a see saw like position. The player then touched the tip of the wood so as to make it lift upward, and then hit it with another long branch of tree/ piece of wood for 10-20 times, as per the decision made among the players before playing. While hitting for the 2nd , 3rd , 4th ....20th time, the player would have to hit from the position where that branch previously fell down. Once the player completed hitting for the required times, he/she would have to come back to the previous position that is, to the hole, by making a sound "ha....uuuuuuu" while holding his/her breath. If he/she was able to reach and fulfil the above criteria, he/she won the game, if not, the other player would get a chance to play in the same process.

CHAPTER 3

STONE GAMES

Mawpoin - This is the Khai-Jaintia version of the popular Indian Seven Stone game, also called the following names in other parts of the country :

- Pithu garam

- Dikori

- Lagoori

- Lingocha (Hyderabad)

- Lingorchya (Maharashtra)

- Pitthu (Haryana)

- Satoliya (Rajasthan)

- Satodiya (Gujarat)

- Yedu Penkulata (Andra Pradesh)

- Dabba Kali (Kerala)

- Ezhu Kallu (Tamil Nadu)

https://www.traditionalgamesindia.com/games-list/satoliya-the-seven-stone/ accessed on 13-08-2023 at 13.37 pm

Mawpoin is a type of game played by children of all ages (usually those approximately below 16years), though even adults can play the game. The game can be played both by male and female. The name "mawpoin" has two meanings - 'maw' which means stones or stone, where the arrangement of stones is one on top of the other, preferably the biggest one at the bottom , which is followed by smaller and smaller stones, and 'poin' means score. The game consists of two teams. The number of players and height of the arranged stones may vary from place to place, that is it can be of any height as per the desire of the players. The shape of the collected stones could be both flat and uneven.

Before the game starts, the players are divided into two teams. Stones are collected and arranged almost like a pyramid, one on top of the other. Then a toss with a coin (or a small flat stone) is made. The team in whose favour the coin or small flat stone comes out, will begin the game by throwing a ball straight at the already arranged stones. In some places, one person will be standing next to the stones and he/she will hit or throw the ball in any direction. The opposite team (opponent) will then try to catch the ball and try to throw it at each member of the other team, not letting them rearrange the stones. If the ball hits a person of the opposite team, then that person is no longer eligible to play, and is considered 'dead' from the team. In some places, the ball is allowed to hit any part of the body, while in some, a rule is made that if only the hand or the head of a team member gets hit, that person can still play and continue the game, which means he/she is not out. The game will end in two ways; either when all the stones are completely rearranged or when all the players have been hit by the ball, and the teams will win and lose respectively. In this way mawpoin is an interesting and most popular indigenous game that is still played by children of all age groups as well as by adults.

Children playing "Mawpoin"

Mawkynting/ Mawkhalai/ Mawsan/Mawdot (five stones)

Different places have different names for this type of game. Some call it mawkynting some call it mawkhalai some mawsan and some mawdot. However the game is the same. It is a type of game which is usually played with five stones. The number of players varies (that is, it can be above two) . Five stones of similar shape (mostly oval) are collected. The game consists of three main steps; the first step is called "khalai" where these five stones are made to spread in a flat surface (flat ground) by gently throwing them from the palm. Then the teams will choose among the spread stones. After the opponent players/player has chosen the stone then, he/ she will have to try to take the stone two each by lifting that chosen stone. While he/she lifts that chosen stone, he/ she will have to try to take away two stones together with the lifted stones. The technique of taking the rested stones differs from person to person. If he/she can finish the step perfectly, then he/she can continue with the next steps,. The next step is called "u ting" where the player will have to lift again one stone of their choice and put back the remaining stones on the ground simultaneously, and take away again the remaining stones from the ground. If the individual completes this step perfectly, then they go to the next round, otherwise he/she is out from the first round. The next step is called "u peh" where the player will have to lift all the 5 stones together and try to let them fall and stay in the palm of the hand. The stones remaining in the palm are caught and counted. The game continues for the next round, depending on the desire of the players. The scores or points are counted from the stones remaining on the palm. One of the rules or conditions in this game is that if a player forgets their previous step, in the next round, they can go for a condition called a "truh" where a player is free to lift the stones, depending upon their desire, but they should lift not less than two stones. After this, the player will again have to lift all the 5 stones and let them fall on the palm(outward) and then throw the stones up and try to catch them with their fingers. Mawkynting is one of the famous indigenous games which are played by children and even adults in the Khasi Hills of Meghalaya. However many children in the urban areas have forgotten the rules and constraints of the game.

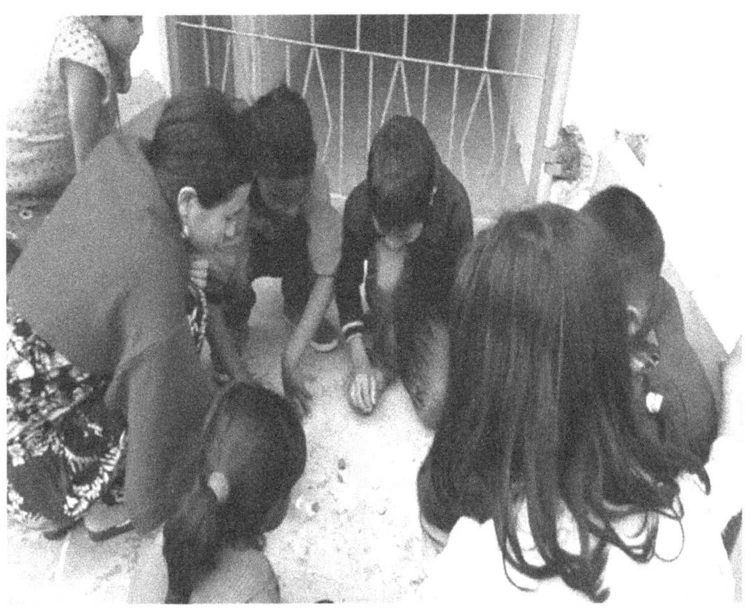

Children playing Mawkynting

Kawang maw pyllon/ iamir maw pyllon

This is a type of indigenous game mostly played by male children. "Kawang" means to throw and "mawpyllon" are small round marbles which are made of clay. Thus the game is about playing with these clay marbles. The number of players can be up to 5. Before the game starts, the players will bet among them on how many marbles they will have to throw and how many to give to the winner. Then a circular hole is made on the ground. And a mark is made which acts as the boundary for throwing. The player who gets to play first will begin the game by throwing the marbles, if the bet was about throwing two marbles, then that player will have to throw two marbles gently into the hole. If both the marbles get inside the hole, then that is taken as null, that is, the player will have to throw the stones again. If one marble gets into the hole and the other lands outside, anywhere on the ground, then the second player will gently throw his/her two marbles into the hole. If his/her two marbles get inside the hole, he/she will have to throw his/her marble towards the marble of the first player, which lies outside the hole. If he/she can let his/her marble collide with the marble of that first player, he/she wins the game. If not, the game will be continued by the third player and so on. If any player wins, the others will have to pay him/her with marbles, depending on the bet made earlier. In this way, this game was played in the past, and known to be popular among children in the Khasi Hills.

CHAPTER 4

FOREIGN INFLUENCED GAMES PLAYED THE MEGHALAYA WAY

Following are some_foreign influenced games played the Meghalaya way:

Soh tyngkoh (hopping on one leg/hop skotch)

This game requires space so as to draw the kinds of tables/blocks for playing.

In this type of game, children use flat stones as material for playing. The game is about jumping on the drawn tables/blocks with one leg lifted. The game begins by deciding who will get to play in the first round. Then a table is drawn and divided into two columns. The tables/blocks are numbered (1,2,3…and so on). In the first step, each child throws their stone on the first block on one side of the table. Then they hop on each block on the other side of the table, coming round to the side where the stone has been placed. Once they reach that stone, they stamp on the stone and kick it outside the table, whereby, in some cases they again stamp on the stone outside the table. Once this is finished, the child throws the stone on the second block of the table and the process goes on like this till all the boxes/rows in the table are covered .

Rules and constraints

1. If the stone does not reach the required table, the player is considered to be out from the first round of the game.

2. If the leg touches the line of the table, then that player is considered to be out from the game.

3. While kicking the stone outside the table, if the player fails to stamp on the stone, then she/he is considered out from the game.

The game ends when there is a winner completing all the rows of the table.

Children playing Soh tyngkoh

Tan tyllai (tug of war)/ la di-kut u sai tyllai

This is like the tug of war game that is played around the world, however it is called indigenous game because the way the game is played in Meghalaya is different and it goes along with a song.

Before the tug of war begins, leaders of the two opposing teams are chosen, as 'king' and 'queen' who will be the leaders of the two teams. These will in turn act as gates or barrier of their respective teams. After being chosen, the two leaders will then join their hands upward in an arch and start singing the game's song, and the other children will enter through this arch, in a queue. Once the song is over, the leaders will catch the last person who is stuck in between them. The song will be sung for many rounds till all the children have chosen sides. Then the leaders will ask each player to choose between the leaders. Once that is done, the player will have to go to the side of their choice . This process will go on till all the players get the chance to choose sides . Then the tug of war begins. They will either pull each others' hands or a rope.

The song sung for choosing participants goes like this

La di-kut u sai tyllai,

Mon la ka mon ka herimai

La dkut la dkut u sai tyllai ban bteng d'u ba thymmai;

Lah ka ksiar ne ka rupa,

Mon sha I ne mon sha nga

La dkut la dkut u sai tyllai ban bteng d'u ba thymmai.

Du du du du du du du du…dam!

(Loosely translated, "the rope is broken, we'll have to repair it by tying it with another rope," whose side would you choose? His/hers or mine?")

Children taking part in Tan Tyllai (tug of war)

Pynshad latom (spinning the top):

This game is mostly played by male children in the Khasi Hills. "Pynshad" means "to spin" and latom means " top," hence the game is about spinning the top and who can stop or topple the spinning top. It is an individual game where the players compete with each other. The top is made from a piece of wood with a nail protruding from the middle of the top. A thread is twirled around the top and pulled out to release the top.

First of all, the players gather together along with their tops or latom, with the aim of destroying the spinning top of the other player. A big circle is drawn for spinning the top. Then the players will decide who will spin the top first. Once the first player starts spinning the top, the others will quickly spin their tops too, by throwing towards the previous top in order to disrupt its spin. The first player will have to protect his top by quickly pulling the top away with the thread. The game will continue and end when there are only two players left who will be fighting amongst each other until one wins.

Rules and constraints:

1. A top should not spin outside the circle. If so, the player will no longer be eligible to stay and play in the game.

2. Once the top is toppled by the other players, that player will no longer be eligible to be in the game.

3. Once the player is able to pull away the top, he is safe and will get the chance to destroy the tops of others.

Ialeh ialuh/ ialeh iarieh(hide and seek)

This is similar to the hide and seek game. Ialeh means to play and iarieh/ialuh means to hide. The game is about hiding and seeking between players who are in the game. The game begins by deciding who will hide and who will seek. The seeker closes their eyes and counts while the other player/s will then hide. Once the others are ready, the seeking process begins. The game will end when all the players get caught. The one who got caught first will then continue the game by seeking. The game will finally end when the players decide for it to end.

Ialeh iarieh (hide and seek)

Shut tin/ kawang tin

Both male and female children can play this game together. "Shut"is colloquial for shoot or kick, "kawang" means to throw/fling and "tin" simply means tin. The number of players varies (i.e it can be above 2). The game is similar to hide and seek. but in addition, children use a bottle to play with. This kind of game, children played outside the house and usually in the backyard. The game begins like this - firstly all the players will come together, then they will decide among them who will seek the other players. Once a decision is made, a small circle is drawn and a bottle is put inside a small circle.in front of the house. One among the players kicks the bottle, while the other players run to the backyard of the house/ building to hide. After he/she kicks the bottle, he/she too runs as fast as he/she can to the backyard of the house, to seek out the others. The seeker will then have to put back the bottle in the circle and begin seeking. If a seeker catches any of the players he/she will have to run back towards the bottle, to assure that he/she caught the player. In the process, the player who got caught too will run as much as he/she can in order to kick back the bottle. If he/she fails to do so, then he/she is out of the game, and the one who got caught in the first or last position will become the seeker. However, if the player who got caught manages to kick back the bottle then he/she is saved and gets the chance to hide again. That is, he/she would have to run again after he/she had kicked back the bottle. There is no specific ending to the game, however the game would end depending upon the desire of the players.

Lehkai marbul (playing with marbles)

It is a kind of indigenous game played mostly by male children of all ages. The game was famous over the past recent years and is still played by children in villages. However, the game is less popular in urban areas. The game is about playing with marbles. Marbles are small rounded beads. The game is played in two ways.

One way is called the "lehkai ia in" and the other way is called "lehkai thri sik"

"Lehkai ia in"

"Lehkai ia in" means to play with the use of the "in". "In" means inside and the "in" is a rounded or rectangular shape drawn on the ground, in which marbles are kept. Firstly, the players decide for how many marbles they will be playing, once decided these marbles are clubbed together and kept inside the "in." Then a line is drawn near the "in." The players then strike their marbles (the one which are not inside the "in") with their fingers and strike the marbles which are inside the 'in.' The person with the marble which is nearer to the line, will be the first player to strike the "in". once the player strikes the "in" he/she should make sure that the marbles inside the "in" and the marble which strikes should not stay inside the "in," if so, he/she is out from the game, but if he/she accomplishes the task, he/she gets the marbles.

"Lehkai thri sik"

"Thri" in context of the game means three, sik means six. This game is played in series. That is the marbles are struck for a number of series. The series goes like this, "three < six < nine < twelve < fif < eight < pass < pot". The beginning of the game is similar to the above game.

Pynher kot kudi (kite flying)

Mostly teenagers of Khasi Hills district play this game. This game was mostly played by male children. "Pynher" means to fly and "kot kudi" means kite. Thus pynher kot kudi simply means flying of kites in the sky. It was one of the popular games in the Khasi hills in the olden times. This game was mostly played during spring season. This game involved skills and physical strength. It is in fact a common game in different parts of the world.

The game was about fighting between flying kites. The children used techniques on how to cut the kites of others in the sky with a thread. One of the common techniques was using the "manja" which in Khasi is called the "khleh manja" where they used flour, powdered glass, rice etc. This paste was coated on the thread, in order to make the thread sharp.

Siat khnam (archery)

Siat khnam (archery)

This is a type of indigenous archery which is still practiced in the Khasi Hills. However today it is known as "teer," as it involves legal betting. Before teer came into the picture, archery was known to be the most popular and enjoyable games among the Khasis, as many people who have trained themselves come from villages to take part in the game. It is an adult game. But to become archers, children were trained from their youth on how to use "khnam"(arrow) and "ryntieh"(bow) to strike the target. The target is called the "skum" (made of dry leaves or grass or straw).

Lehkai tap khmat

Tap khmat means blind fold. It is a type of game where the player, who is the chaser, will be blind folded and made to search for the other players. The children hit the chaser with objects such as metal and tin to catch the chaser's attention. The game ends when the chaser catches all the players.

Kynthih jri

This game is mostly played by female children of all ages. The game is similar to sports like high jump etc., however the rules and way of playing are different. Till today, this game is still played by children in most places of the Khasi Hills. This game involves physical strength, where all the levels involve movement of parts of the body. The raw material used are small rubber bands which are tied/joined together to form a long string.

The game begins by dividing the players into teams (the number of teams varies, it depends upon the decision of the players). The team that wins the toss will get to play first. The game however can be played individually also, as long as there is a rubber string. The game is divided into different levels and each level, all the player will have to perform and finish smoothly. A rubber is tied to walls or poles, from one end to the other end. The height of the string is increased as the game progresses. The following are the levels of the game:

> **Level 1:** Khohsiew (The knee)/ cross: This is the first and foremost level. It is called khohsiew (the knee) because the height of the rubber is measured from the ground to the knee. It is also called cross because each player will have to jump and cross their leg simultaneously for 3 to 6 times

> **Level 2:** ka jum (high jump): The height of the rubber is then measured from the ground to the thigh. This is the second level where the player/s will have to jump above the rubber without touching it for 2-3 times depending on the decision of the player. It is similar to a high jump.

> **Level 3:** ka bum(butt): The height of the rubber is lifted to the butt/bottom. This is the third level where players will have to jump from one side to the other side provided they don't touch the rubber for 2-3 times depending on the decision of the players.

> **Level 4:** syngkai (hips): the height is lifted to the hips. In this level, the player can move from one side of the rubber to the other side by pulling the rubber with one leg, for 2-3 times, depending on the decision of the players.

> **Level 5:** shadem(chest): the height of the rubber is lifted to the chest. In this level, the player will have to do exactly as the previous level.

> **Level 6:** tmoh(chin): the height of the rubber is now lifted to the chin. In this level the player will do a

backward leg cross by firstly pulling the rubber by one leg, for 3-6 times, depending on the decision of the players.

> **Level 7:** lbong(thigh): the height of the rubber is now reduced back to the thigh. This level is also called high cross, where the player will have to do again a leg cross for 2-3 times, depending on the decision of the players.

> **Level 8:** ka spid(speed): the height of the rubber is, reduced to the knee. In this level the player will have to do a fast jump provided that both the legs should not be separated, from one side of the rubber to the other side for 3-6 times, depending on the decision of the players.

> **Level 9:** Sohtyngkoh(hop on one leg): the height of the rubber remains on the knee. This is the last level. In this level the player will have to hop on one leg from one side to the other for 3- 6 times, depending on the decision of the players.

Rules and constraints of the game:

1. A player will not be eligible to play the next level if he/she does not complete the previous level.

2. A player will have to complete all the levels in order to win the game.

3. If the player fails to complete at one level, then the second time he/she gets to play, he/she will be allowed to continue with that level that he/she lost in the previous game.

This game is still played by children in schools, village play grounds and so on.

Children playing "kynthih jri"

Hai-iu

Hai-iu can be played both by male and female children but is mostly played by female children. In some places this game is still common but played irregularly. The game consists of two rounds.   In this game, the players will have to make a sound while holding their breath and chasing the opponents.

The game begins by dividing the players into two teams. A circle is drawn which acts as a home or safe place or a boundary for the team which will have to chase. The team that wins the toss will begin the game, by chasing the opposing team. Before chasing, the team who will chase will give different names to each player (eg. apple for one player, mango for the other etc..) then they will ask the opponent to choose among the options of names given. Once the opposing team chooses any of the players, that player will then chase the members of the opposite team by making the sound "hai…….uuuuuu……" while holding their breath. The game will end in two ways; either all the players of one team will get the chance to chase members of the other team or they are defeated or 'dead'.

Rules and constraints of the game

1. In the first round, the first team will chase the opposite team and in the second round the opposite team will have to chase the first team.

2. Once the player starts chasing, he/she will have to make the sound while holding their breath.

3. While chasing, he/she should adjust his/her breath so as he/she can reach home safely.

4. If the chaser fails to make the sound continuously, the opponent team can catch back the chaser and he/she will not be eligible to play in the game. That means he/she is dead from the game.

5. If the chaser fails to make a continuous sound, but is able to get to the circle, he/she is safe and eligible to play in the game.

6. If the chaser is able to catch a player from the opposite team, then that player is dead from the game.

7. If the first team is able to catch all the players of the opposite teams, then that team gets one point. If not, then they will have to try to catch the players of the opposite team in the second round, when they will be chasing the opposite team.

8. If both the teams are not able to catch all the players of the opposite team, then there is a tie.

9. If there is a tie between the teams, the teams will again play from the beginning.

Children playing Hai-iu

Khiew jakai

This is also one of the popular games played in the olden times. This type of game was played during a family visit, or family reunion, and even among children in the neighbourhood. This game can be played by both male and female, though female children prefer to play this kind of game more.

This game involved a kind of role playing. In other words children who participated in the game took up their own character such as that of a mother, a father, a son/daughter and as friend and so on, depending on the number of participants. The game had the various characters involving in daily household and professional activities like cooking, attending occasions like birthday party or wedding etc. as per the decision of the participants in the game. While playing, most children used raw materials like clothes, stones, sand, water , leaves, flowers and anything that was easy to get from mother earth.

This type of game was played in two ways. One way was playing in a group and the other was individually. Today, it is not so common.

Lehkai bol ha mawjyngkieng(playing ball on steps)

It is a type of indigenous game mostly played by female children and teenagers (approx. 16years below). "lehkai bol" means playing with a ball and "mawjyngkieng" means steps or staircases. Till today, this type of game is still played by children in some of the places of Khasi Hills District. This game involves strength and movement of the hands. The number of players may vary. The raw materials used are any kind of ball (i.e either a plastic ball or a rubber ball) and steps/stairs. This type of game, children were likely to play in schools or anywhere, provided there are steps/stairs in it. The game is about bouncing the ball on each step. However there are rules and constraints for playing such game. The following are the rules and constraints of the game:

Rules and constraints

1. Each player will have to bounce and catch the ball one time on each step and continue till the ball has been bounced on all the pre chosen steps. The number of steps for bouncing(marked steps) may vary; it can be between 5-6 or 7-8 steps. Once the player reaches the upper most marked steps he/she will have to come back to the lower most step, known as backward bouncing.

2. While the player bounces and catches the ball on each step, he/she should stand/ remain in constant position.

3. The player is out if he/she fails or misses a steps, that is for example if he/she bounces the ball on step number 7 instead of 5 or 6 or when he/she is unable to catch the ball after each bounce.

4. If the player completes bouncing the ball on all the marked steps, he/she gets to move his/her position to the next step. And the process goes on till the player reaches to the top most marked step.

5. Once the player reaches the top most step, he/she wins the game.

In some places, children continue the game by catching the bouncing ball with only one hand from the first step right up to the top.

Puh syiar

This game is mostly played by children above 9 -10 years. This game was mostly played by male children. "puh syiar" means chicken fight. It is so called because the way of playing resembles a chicken fight. This game was mostly popular in the olden times, however today few people still remember the game and the way it was played. There was no specific number of players for playing the game. The more the number of players, the more fun the game. This game was about fighting against each other by pushing with one side of the shoulder.

Rules and constraints

1) Firstly, a circle is drawn on the ground. The players gather inside the circle with one hand at the back and standing on one foot.

2) One will act as a judge to supervise the players.

3) Once the judge announces for the game to start, the players will hop and try to push against each other with one side of their shoulder till the other player falls down or goes out of the circle.

4) While the game is going on, the players cannot move their hands, that is - one hand should remain at the back. And the lifted foot should not touch the ground.

5) The game ends when there is only one player left in the circle.

Children playing the game "puhsyiar"

Shong syntuid

Shong mean to sit and syntuid means to slide. It is a type of game which children usually play on a slope using either a piece of wood plank called "lyntang" or big cardboard as a sliding object. There is no winning and losing in this game, but it is a source of fun for children.

CHAPTER 5

Dat Lawakor

Dat- lawakor is a traditional game, similar to football, played during the Behdienkhlam festival of the Jaintias. According to Dr. Omarlin Kyndiah ,"Behdeinkhlam is an occasion that brings the Niaw Wasa closer to God and it also explains the concept of the creation of a community and its religion: Niamtre. Behdeinkhlam is usually celebrated during the high monsoon and after sowing, rites and rituals are also performed to drive away the evil spirits of plague and pestilence". Behdeinkhlam festival is one of the religious festivals among the Pnar (Jaintia) tribal community in the Jaintia hills of Meghalaya, particularly in Jowai, Tuber and Ialong. It is the most important and colourful festival of the followers of Niamtre, in the Jaintia Hills, which is celebrated mid- July every year, after the sowing of paddy is over. The word Behdeinkhlam is a combination of the two Pnar words 'Behdein' and *'khlam'*. The term *'behdein'* laterally means "to drive away/chase off" and *'khlam'* means "plague." Thus the word Behdeinkhlam means "to drive away/chase off plague." According to Mr. Puramon Kynjing, the festival was celebrated since time immemorial and its origin may be traced back to the time when the four heavenly sisters of the Raij viz: *Ka Bon, Ka Tein, Ka Wet and Ka Doh* first came down from heaven to earth and settled at a place which is today known as "Jowai.."The ceremony and rituals are carried out for three days and on the afternoon of the last day, people gather in a place called *Aitnar* where both young and old dance to the tunes of musical pipes and drums. The Behdeinkhlam itself is the religious festival whereby various rituals are performed, procession of the faithful is taken out in the town and the Rots (chariots/Idols) are immersed in the stream. TheDat Lawakor is a game which culminates the Behdeinkhlam festival. The game is played in the context of religious festival in honour of the 'Syiem Rymaw' (Mother Earth) our womb of life. It is about invoking of Syiem Rymaw's blessings for good harvest. It is symbolic to each and everyone who resides in Jowai, especially farmers.

As a part of the celebration, a game called Dat Lawakor, which is similar to football, is held between the residents of the northern side of Jowai and the southern side, each team trying to score a goal with a wooden ball. The meaning of the game is derived from the word 'Lawakor' which is a wooden ball made from bamboo roots. "Dat Lawakor is not simply a game but also a devotional act of propitiation to mother earth (*KaSyiemRymaw*) – the mother of all living things," according to Dawmanchuh Lamar. The outcome of the game is a kind of prediction of the success or failure of the crop harvest. The one to score first is the winner and it is also believed that the winner would have a bumper harvest. Dat Lawakor is the game that used to be played by the people of Seinraij Jowai, on the last day of Behdeinkhlam festival, which is held every year around the month of June or July. The festival ends with the final salutation to the divine powers, when the women of the tribe offer sacrificial food to the Almighty.

The game is played between two teams i.e. the upper side and lower side. The members who are going to participate in this game should be six a side (5 players + U Langdoh for

Pynthorwah & 5 players + U Sangot for Pynthornein) . Since the game is played to seek the blessing of 'Syiem Rymaw' for beautiful harvest, it is played between the settlers of Pynthornein (upper valley) and Pynthorwah (lower valley).

The lower or valley side (Pynthorwah) is led by *'U Langdoh'* (i.e. from the clan of Doh) while the upper valley side (Pynthornein) is led by *'U SangotPaswet'* (i.e. from the clan of Wet) and each team tries to score a goal with a wooden ball. The one to score first is the winner and it is also believed that the winner would have a bumper harvest. The game is always played under the supervision of *'U Dalloi'*. Through this game it is believed that if the *Langdoh's* team wins the match, paddy will grow abundantly at Pynthor- wah and if the *Sangot – Pasweth's* team wins the match, then rice will grow abundantly at Pynthor – Nein.

Kynting Khnong

Chariots/Rots

Significance of the game

The significance of the game is that it is a platform for the faithful to get together and enjoy the gaiety of the festival. It is a natural practice of the agrarian Pnar society to perform a religious festival during high monsoon and after sowing season. Thus the game 'Datlawakor' is played to seek the blessings of 'Syiem Rymaw' (Mother Earth) for beautiful harvest. It is a symbol of Mother Nature's blessing upon man (human beings) in fulfillment of God's command.

Khnongs

According to Dawmanchuh Lamar, Behdeinkhlam bears the witness in testifying the strong belief of the people on the real God, who is addressed as U Blai (God), *U Tre Kynrad, U Syiem Blai*. It signifies the undiluted spirit of reverence towards nature and Mother Earth. It provides one with information on the roles of Mother Earth as the *Ka Syiem Um Ka Syiem Wah*(the queen of water), the *Ka Syiem Khyndaw Ka Syiem Chyiap* (the queen of the soils) that shelters and feeds all living entities on earth and reminds one of one's solemn duties towards her. This festival has a strong relationship with agriculture and *Ka Sngi Thoh Langdoh* is similar to the 'Earth Day' or Environment Day as it is celebrated in the 21st century world. It is noted that on this day, no one is allowed to work in the field or to burn any rubbish in one's garden.

Process of Dat Lawakor

La-wakor is a wooden ball used in Dat lawakor and it is to be kept in the custody of the Pyrbot clan. Traditionally it is also mandatory for the *U Sangot Pakyntein* to go and collect the La-wa-kor from the Pyrbot clan on the day of the festival, and to also bring it to the teams. It is also his duty to return it to its rightful custodian. It is the duty of the Dalloi to conduct and preside over the proceedings of Ka Dat la-wa-kor. For instance, if it falls in a pit or a drain, it is the duty of his assistant (U Chutia) to pick up and hand it over to the *U Dalloi* for the resumption of the religious game.

The ball

Items Required

i) Lawakor – wooden ball

Rules & Regulations

The rules and regulations of this game are:

i) No specific age group

ii) Gender: only male participants.

iii) No time limit

iv) No one is allowed to wear shoes

v) No one can touch the ball except U Sangot , and

vi) The declaration will be given by the Dalloi.

Problems

a. No special ground is prepared for this game and it is just played along the street.

b. The people have to go wherever the ball goes.

Acknowledgements

The authors acknowledge the wise advice of the following key people, on various aspects of the Behdeinkhlam festival and Dat Lawakor.

Dr. OmarlinKyndiah:

He is the General Secretary, Sein Raij Niamtre Shillong, (the congregation of the indigenous faith settled in Shillong), who is also an Associate Professor and Head of the Department of Biochemistry, St. Edmund's College, Shillong.

Mr. Puramon Kynjing (Dalloi/Traditional chief):

He is one of the traditional chiefs of the Behdeinkhlam festival. He plays the most important role in the Behdeinkhlam festival. As the religious head, he presides over the proceedings of all the activities before, during and after the event.

Mr. Rangpher Rynjah:

He is an important member of the indigenous religious group, the Seng Khasi, in Shillong. He is also one of the Semi-Professional Assistants in-charge of the Reference section in the Central Library, NEHU, Shillong.

Dr. H.C Pakyntein:

He is known as *U Sangot* (from the clan of Tein) of the Elaka Jowai and he is also one of the practitioners of Herbal medicine.

Mr. O.R. Challam:

He is the President of Seinraij, Jowai. He is a retired Associate Professor and former Head of the History Department at Kiang Nangbah Government. College, Jowai.

CHAPTER 6

SUGGESTIONS & CONCLUSION

Suggestions

Some of the games mentioned here were popular in the past, while some remain popular till today. Playing these games helps both the young and old physically as well as mentally. People unite with others, which in turn unites the community itself. However, most children of today's generation are not aware about the existence of indigenous games of the community, because they were not taught and also because of the onslaught of modern games, especially online games.

The other threat to indigenous knowledge is that it is transmitted by word of mouth (orally). When the experts die, the knowledge dies along with them. Therefore it is important to preserve the games before they get extinct, especially through print and audio visual documentation. Indigenous games, being such vital parts of the life of the indigenous people, it is important to document and preserve such games on an individual and corporate basis. The government , sports associations, religious groups and even academic institutions should hold programmes from time to time, where these games can be played by children who can also learn about the significance of these games. Libraries too can play a major role in preserving indigenous games.

They can do so by identifying, collecting, preserving and disseminating such knowledge to the public. With today's advanced technology, it becomes easier to preserve the indigenous knowledge on indigenous games. Libraries should collaborate with indigenous people in order to acquire, store and make indigenous knowledge accessible. They should also publicise the value and contribution of indigenous games to the indigenous as well as non indigenous people. Libraries should also collaborate with the government, to ensure that the government can provide funds for preserving indigenous knowledge. Many of the respondents to this study were of the opinion that it is important to preserve indigenous games as they are not expensive (that is, the materials used in each game are available in the immediate surroundings) and that they are healthy games.

Problems relating to indigenous games played in the Khasi and Jaintia Hills Districts of Meghalaya

According to the respondents, indigenous games in the Khasi and Jaintia hills face the following threats:

> Urbanisation: Spaces for playing any games are gradually decreasing due to urbanisation.

> Electronic games, social media: with the advance of technology, children get influenced by media such as television, online and offline games. Therefore, they prefer to spend most of their time on these than playing physically.

Limitations of the Study

The information on the indigenous games was gathered from the identified key people who have some broad ideas about the games. However, there were some issues encountered during the findings, as many people tend to forget the different processes and even names of some of the games. In addition, photographs of some of the games could not be taken.

Conclusion

Indigenous games, while being unique, also help children physically as well as mentally. Through such games, children unite with other children, which in turn unites the community itself. However most children of today's generation, are not aware about the existence of indigenous games of their communities, either because they were never taught about such games or because they don't value the significance of such games, thinking instead that online games are better. This study attempted to document some indigenous games played in the Khasi and Jaintia Hills of Meghalaya, India. Most of these games were or are played in other districts of Meghalaya as well. The results of this study, despite the shortcomings, may help bring some awareness on such games to all readers and hopefully lead to other such studies as well.

REFERENCES AND BIBLIOGRAPHY

1. Ajibade, L.T. (2003) A methodology for the collection and evaluation for farmer's indigenous environmental knowledge in developing countries. Indilinga: *African Journal of Indigenous Knowledge system*, 2, 37 -44.

2. Bayeck, R. Y. (2017) A review of five African board games: is there any educational potential?. *Cambridge Journal of Education*, 1(1), 1469-3577. Retrieved 1 March, 2018, from https://doi.org/10.1080/030576 4X.2017.137167

3. Bio-Resource Development Centre, Shillong, Meghalaya, https://megbrdc.nic.in/initiatives_ documentation_of_traditional_best_practices.html

4. Camacho et al. (2016) Indigenous knowledge and practices for the sustainable management of Ifugao forests in Cordillera, *Philippines International Journal of Biodiversity Science, Ecosystem Services & Management* , 12(1-2), 5-13.

5. Cambridgeorg. (2018). Cambridgeorg. Retrieved 15 February, 2018, from https://dictionary.cambridge.org/ dictionary/english/game

6. Defining-indigenous-knowledge. (2018). Defining-indigenous-knowledgehtml. Retrieved 31 March, 2018, from http://www.theory-of-knowledge. net>defining-indigenous-knowledge.html

7. Dolphen, I. (2014) Learning language and culture through indigenous knowledge: A case study of teaching a minority language (Mon) in a majority language (Thai) school setting. *Procedia - Social and Behavioral Sciences* , 134(236). Retrieved 31 March, 2018, from https://www.sciencedirect.com/science/article/pii/S1877042814031462

8. Ferreira, M. B. R. (2014) " Indigenous games: A struggle between past and present," *ICSSPE Bulletin Journal of Sport Science and Physical Education,* No 67, p.48

9. Fondahl, G. (2015) Indigenous peoples in the new Arctic. **In** Evengård, B, Larsen, J.N & Paasche Q. (Eds), **The new Arctic** (pp. 7-22). Switzerland: Springer, Cham

10. Fox, E.A. (2005) The role of digital libraries in moving toward knowledge environments. **In** Hemmje,, M, Niederee, C & Risse, T (Eds), **From integrated publication and information systems to information and knowledge environments,** pp. 96-106. Berlin: Springer.

11. International Federation of Library Associations and Institutions (2008). IFLA statement on indigenous traditional knowledge. Available: http://www.ifla.org/publications/ifla-statement-on-indigenous-traditional-knowledge

12. Ipccch. (2018) Ipccch. Retrieved 31 March, 2018, from https://www.ipcc.ch/publication-and-data/ar4/wgz/en/ch9s9-6-2.html

13. Lamar, D. (2015) An insight into Behdeinkhlam festival. Shillong: Eastern Panorama.

14. Magga. O. H. (2005) Indigenous knowledge system – the true roots of humanism. *World library and Information congress.*71st IFLA General conference and council. Libraries – A voyage of discovery.

15. Nafaforestryorg. (2018). Nafaforestryorg. Retrieved 25 February, 2018, from http://nafaforestry.org/forest_home/documents/TKdefs-FH-19dec06.pdf

16. Nakashima,D. & Roue, M. (2002). Indigenous knowledge, people and sustainable practices.Vol.5.314-324

17. Nakata et al. (2013). Indigenous knowledge, the library and information service sector, and protocols.*Australian Academic & Research Libraries,* 36(2), 7-21. Retrieved 8 may, 2018, from https://doi.org/10.1080/00048623.2005.1072124

18. Ndiko, L. (2018) "*Indigenous Games,*" Blog in https://www.etacollege.com/indigenous-games/

19. Nwabueze ,A. (2010). The role of libraries in the preservation and accessibility of indigenous knowledge in the Niger delta region of Nigeria. *Library Philosophy and practice (e-journal).*387. http://digitalcommons.unl.edu/libphilprac/387

20. Nwabueze, A. (2018) Digital Commons @University of Nebraska - Lincoln. Retrieved 4 March, 2018, from https://digitalcommons.unl.edu/libphilprac/387/

21. Nyong, A. Adesina, F. & Elasha, B.O. (2007). The value of indigenous knowledge in climate change mitigation and adaptation strategies in the African Sahel. *Mitigation and Adaptation Strategies for Global Change,* 12(5), 787–797.

22. Okore (2009) The role of libraries in the preservation of indigenous knowledge in Primary healthcare in Nigeria.*International Journal of Digital Library services,* 5(2), 26-30.

23. Sarah, E.A. (2015) The role of libraries in preserving and promoting indigenous knowledge in primary healthcare in Nigeria. *International journal of digital library services,* 5(2), 43-54.

24. Singh, S.R. & Singh, N. S. (2012) Traditional sports and martial arts of Meghalaya. *International journal of innovative research and development,* 1(9), 690-698.

25. Speaonlineca. (2018) Speaonlineca. Retrieved 20 february, 2018, from https://www.speaonline.ca/uploads/3/8/2/9/38299825/indiginous_games_handout_by_cole_wilson.pdf

26. Srsagovza. (2018) Srsagovza. 5 march, 2018, from http://www.srsa.gov.za/pebble.asp?relid=167

27. Stevans,A.(2008) A different way of knowing: Tools and strategies for managing indigenous knowledge. Vol.58,(1),25-33.

28. UNESCOorg.(2008) Unescoorg. Retrieved 24 march, 2018, from http://www.unesco.org/new/en/natural-science/priority-areas/links/related-information/what-is-local-and-indigenous-knowledge/

29. World Bank.(1998) Indigenous knowledge for development: A framework for action, 1-49. Retrieved from http://www.worldbank.org

30. Worldbankorg. (2018). World Bank. Retrieved 31 March, 2018, from http://www.worldbank.org/en/topic/indigenouspeople

31. World Intellectual Property Organization (WIPO) (2001) Intellectual property needs and expectations of traditional knowledge holders. Report on fact-finding missions on intellectual property and traditional knowledge 1998-1999, WIPO, Geneva, 2001, p23 at http://www.wipo.int/tk/en/tk/ffm/report/final/pdf/part1.pdf

32. Www.unorg. (2018). WwwUNorg. Retrieved 15 march, 2018, from https://www.UN.org/development/desa/indigenous-peoples/about-us-html

33. http://www.theshillongtimes.com/2016/07/02/festival-tourism-vis-a-vis-religious-festivals/

34. http://raiot.in/behdieinkhlam-trivia-for-non-pnars/

35. http://indpaedia.com/ind/index.php/Behdienkhlam_Festival

About the Authors

Andriana Pyngrope

Andriana, passed her Masters of Library and Information Science, North Eastern Hill University, Shillong in August-2018

She is presently Cluster Coordinator Bosco Integrated Development Society implementing National Rural Livelihood Mission at Mawpat C & RD Block where she involves in activities such as the following :.

- Coordinates the work of grass root institutions including sustainable development and imparts training.

- Prepares statistic and responds to the funding and funding expenditure of the SHGs, VOs.

- Generates monthly, quarterly and yearly reports.

- Provides network between community and financial institution.

- Audits

- Schedules awareness programmes in villages.

- Monthly and Annual Planning.

Bikika Laloo Tariang

She is a teacher and writer. She has been Lecturer in the Department of Library and Information Science, North Eastern Hill University (NEHU), Shillong since 1996 and is presently Professor in the Department. She completed her schooling from Loreto Convent, Shillong; B.A. in Political Science from St. Mary's College, Shillong; M.Lib.I.Sc. from NEHU, Shillong; Ph.D. from Gauhati University, Assam and also has an M.A. in English from Indira Gandhi National Open University (IGNOU).

Her published work includes two books - "*Information Needs, Information Seeking Behaviour and Users,*" and "*Essays on Library and Information Science Education,*" both published by Ess Ess Publications, New Delhi; a collection of English short stories titled, "*Dad and the Salesman,*" published by Writers Workshop, Kolkata; a collection of English poems titled, "*Empty Lives,*" and a collection of Khasi poems titled, "*Jingim Ba Suda,*" both printed by Rilum Press, Shillong. She has also authored "*Mandatory poison and other Shillong things,*" a travel guide published by Notion Press. Her articles have appeared in professional journals, Christian magazines and local newspapers. She has also presented academic and socially relevant papers at local, national and international meetings. Eight scholars have obtained their PhDs while six others are pursuing their PhDs under her supervision. She has completed two terms as Head of the Department of Library and Information Science, North Eastern Hill University (NEHU), Shillong and has been Dean in charge of the School of Economics, Management and Information Science (SEMIS) from time to time since 2022, in the absence of the Dean.

She is life member of the *Indian Library Association* (ILA), *Indian Association of Teachers of Library and Information*

Science (IATLIS), *All India Poetess Conference,* and associate life member of the *Poetry Society of India.* She is also a member of the *North Eastern Hill University Teachers' Association* (NEHUTA) and the *Meghalaya Tribal Teachers Association (*METTA*).*

Rumika Talang

Rumika is Library Assistant in Shangpung College, Jaintia Hills, where she interacts with students and Faculty members and performs library functions and services. She has a degree in Biotechnology from Nandha Arts and Science College, Erode; a degree in M.Lib.I.Sc. from the North Eastern Hill University, Shillong and has also completed a PGDCA from the Jaintia Institute of Technology.

www.ingramcontent.com/pod-product-compliance
Lightning Source LLC
LaVergne TN
LVHW051056180726
843512LV00019B/1492